NATIONAL GEOGRAPHIC

T0288421

Fight the Invaders!

PIONEER EDITION

By Lana Costantini and Kirsten Weir

CONTENTS

THE INVADERS

Armies of creatures are on the move. They kill the animals and plants that get in their way. Is there any way to stop them?

By Lana Costantini

Giant cane toad

A crocodile and a huge cane toad come face-to-face. The croc eats the toad. Soon, the croc is dead, too. Why? It ate a deadly **invader**.

Cane toads cause trouble. People took them to Australia to eat beetles. Instead, the toads ate *everything*.

As the croc found out, cane toads are poisonous. They have few enemies. Now, cane toads are all over northeast Australia. They gobble up insects, frogs, and birds' eggs. Native animals may have nothing left to eat.

Aliens Among Us

Alien species are taking over. These aliens are from Earth! Yet they are moving into places they don't belong.

In their homes, the animals fit in. The balance between predators and prey is right. But when a new species moves in, it can ruin the balance.

How do invaders reach their new homes? People sometimes move plants and animals on purpose. Some invaders ride on ships and planes. When pets get too big, people set them free.

Many invaders thrive in their new homes. They may have few or no enemies. Their numbers grow quickly.

Munch Break. *Up to 30 million nutria live in Louisiana's wetlands.*

Rodents on the Run

Nutria are rodents the size of a small dog. In the 1930s, people brought them from South America. People wanted to raise nutria for fur. Some nutria escaped.

Now, millions of nutria are destroying U.S. wetlands. They munch on wild grasses. They rip out plants by their roots. Then soil washes away. With no soil, new plants can't grow. That leaves no place for animals to hide or make nests.

Lion of the Sea

Red lionfish are great hunters. They sometimes eat 20 fish in just 30 minutes. That's a problem.

Lionfish live naturally in the South Pacific Ocean. There, smaller fish know how to avoid them. Some larger fish there even eat lionfish.

In the Atlantic Ocean, lionfish have no enemies. They can kill most of the fish in a coral reef.

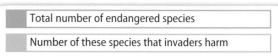

Total number of endangered species

Number of these species that invaders harm

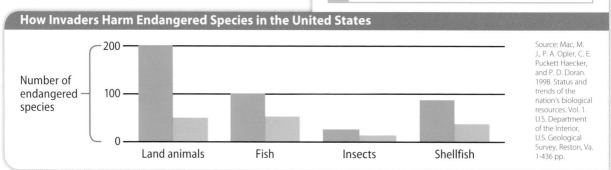

How Invaders Harm Endangered Species in the United States

Number of endangered species

200

100

0

Land animals | Fish | Insects | Shellfish

Source: Mac, M. J., P. A. Opler, C. E. Puckett Haecker, and P. D. Doran. 1998. Status and trends of the nation's biological resources. Vol. 1. U.S. Department of the Interior, U.S. Geological Survey, Reston, Va. 1-436 pp.

Hungry Lions. *Scientists say lionfish eat all the time. That's bad news for other fish.*

Killer Beetles

In Michigan, bug traps catch a killer beetle. It's the emerald ash borer. This green bug is from Asia. It was first seen in Michigan in 2002.

Ash borers lay eggs in the bark of ash trees. The hatchlings eat the inner part of the bark. Without that bark, the tree dies. The ash borer has killed over 30 million ash trees. That's just in Michigan!

Tree Pest. *The emerald ash borer came from Asia. It has spread to ten U.S. states and parts of Canada.*

People Fight Back

How can we stop the invaders? Keep animals and plants from leaving their homes! Once invaders arrive, they are hard to stop.

Australians have a new weapon to fight cane toads. It's the lavender beetle. If a toad eats a beetle, both die.

People set traps to catch nutria and ash borers. Lionfish are harder to catch. But people can't give up! If we don't stop these invaders, who will?

WORDWISE

alien: belonging to a different place, foreign

invader: animal that lives in a place where it doesn't belong

TINY INVADERS

BY KIRSTEN WEIR

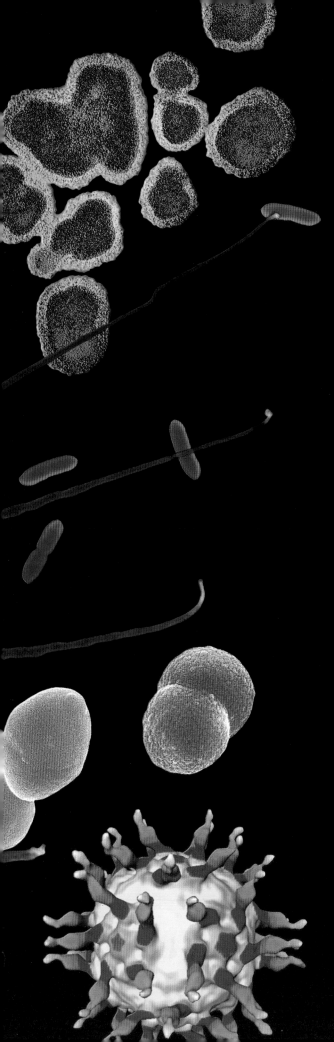

Have you ever been sick?

If so, then you have been invaded! That's right. When you get sick, tiny germs invade your body. Sound scary? Don't worry. Your body works hard to fight them. Read on to find out how.

A World of Germs

The germs that make you sick are everywhere. They are sitting on your desk. They are hiding on this page. They are in the air that you breathe.

Today, germs get around faster than ever. How? For one thing, people take more trips. They take germs with them.

There's another reason germs are spreading. Earth is heating up. This lets animals spread to new places.

Take mosquitoes, for example. They are moving into warmer areas. They often carry germs. When they bite you, those germs can make you sick.

Under Your Skin

How can you protect yourself? Your first defense is your skin. It blocks germs called **viruses**. Viruses cause the flu and chickenpox.

Your skin also blocks bacteria. Some bacteria are good. Others can make you sick. Bacteria can cause sore throats and ear infections.

Sometimes germs get past your skin. They creep through cuts. They ride on food. They can also enter your body through your nose or mouth.

Fighting Back

You can fight these tiny invaders. Start by washing your hands with soap and water. Soap kills many germs. Water washes them away.

Washing your hands isn't always enough. Never fear! Your **immune system** will help. How?

Special cells patrol your body. They eat germs! Other cells make **antibodies**. Antibodies stick to germs. Some antibodies keep germs from making you sick. Others help your body find and kill germs.

After a germ is killed, the antibodies stay in your body. That way you usually will not get the same illness twice.

8

Getting Your Shots

Sometimes the immune system needs help. That's where medicines called vaccines come in.

A vaccine contains killed or weakened germs. They cause you to make antibodies. If the same germ shows up again, antibodies attack it.

Kids can get sick more often than adults. That's because kids haven't been **exposed** to as many germs.

Diseases spread easily. It's a good thing your skin and immune system keep working to protect you.

From the Floor to Your Sandwich

You drop a piece of bread on the floor. But you pick it up within five seconds. Is the bread still safe to eat? No! Bacteria move from the floor to the bread immediately. How many bacteria stick? That depends on how long the bacteria have been on the floor.

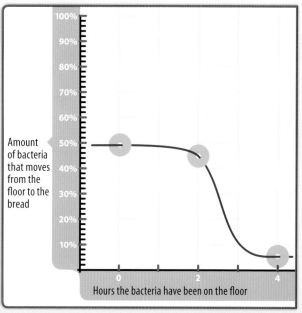

Amount of bacteria that moves from the floor to the bread

Hours the bacteria have been on the floor

Source: Dawson, P., I. Han, M. Cox, C. Black, and L. Simmons, "Residence time and food contact time effects on transfer of *Salmonella* Typhimurium from tile, wood and carpet: testing the five-second rule," *Journal of Applied Microbiology* 102 (2007): 945.

On the Hunt.
The large pink cell is hunting the green bacteria.

Wordwise

antibody: substance that attacks invaders in your body

exposed: made open to something

immune system: parts of your body that fight disease

virus: germ that can live only inside an animal or plant

FIGHTING BACK

Your skin and your cells help protect you from germs. This diagram shows how.

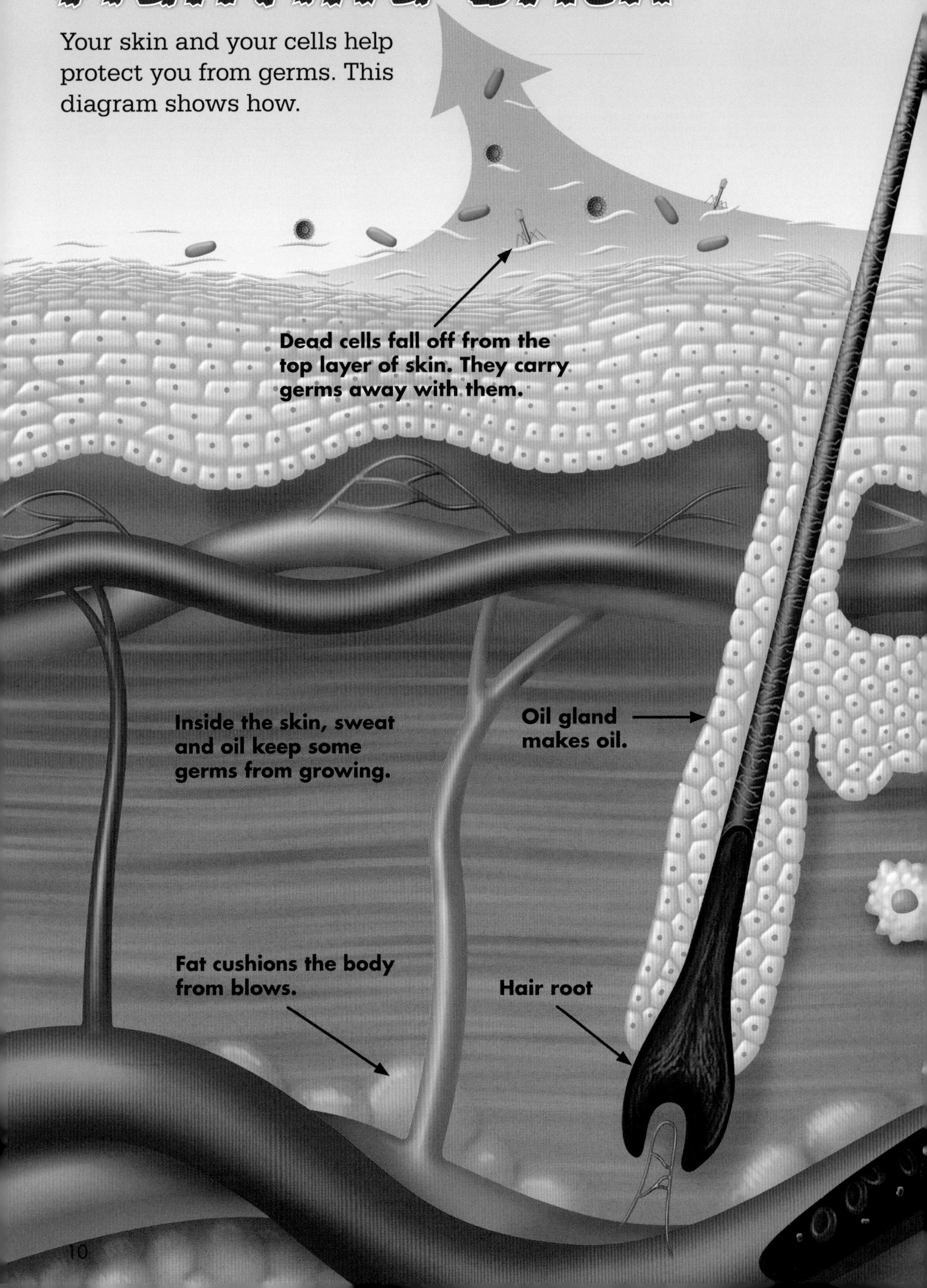

Dead cells fall off from the top layer of skin. They carry germs away with them.

Inside the skin, sweat and oil keep some germs from growing.

Oil gland makes oil.

Fat cushions the body from blows.

Hair root

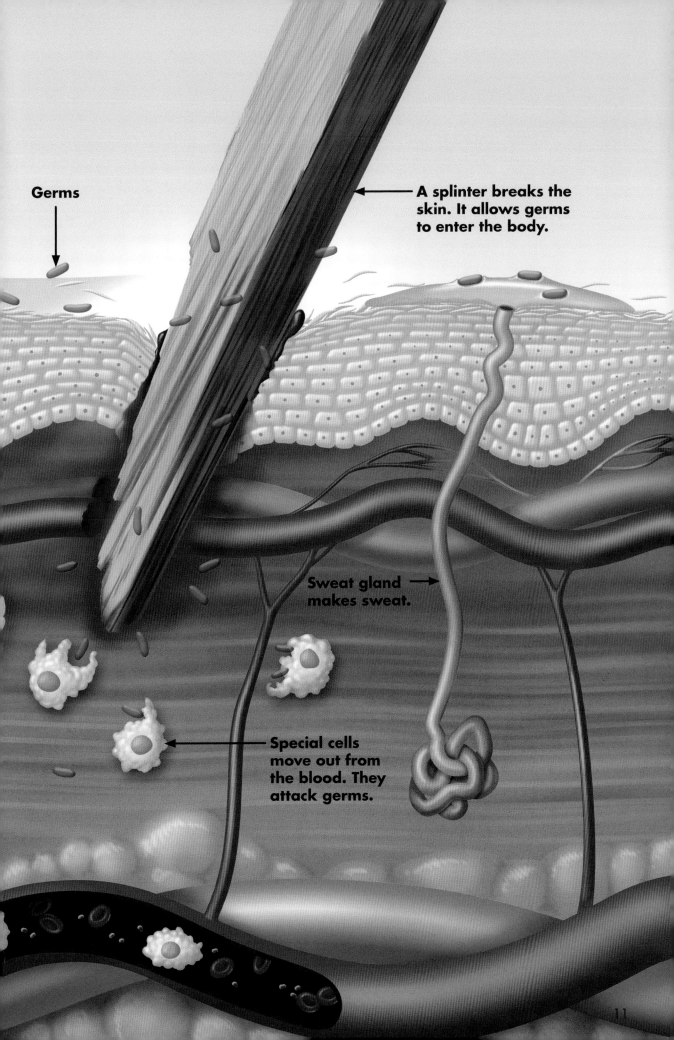

Germs

A splinter breaks the skin. It allows germs to enter the body.

Sweat gland makes sweat.

Special cells move out from the blood. They attack germs.

11

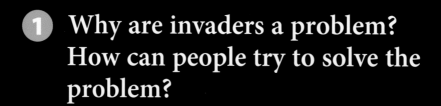

Invasion!

Fight back! Show what you've learned about invaders.

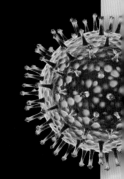

1 Why are invaders a problem? How can people try to solve the problem?

2 Look at the graph on page 4. What living things do invaders harm most?

3 Why do germs spread more quickly now?

4 How does your body fight germs? How do you fight germs with your choices?

5 How are lavender beetles and antibodies the same?

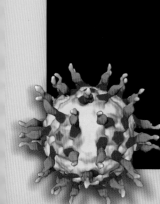